BICYCLES

EVERYDAY INVENTIONS

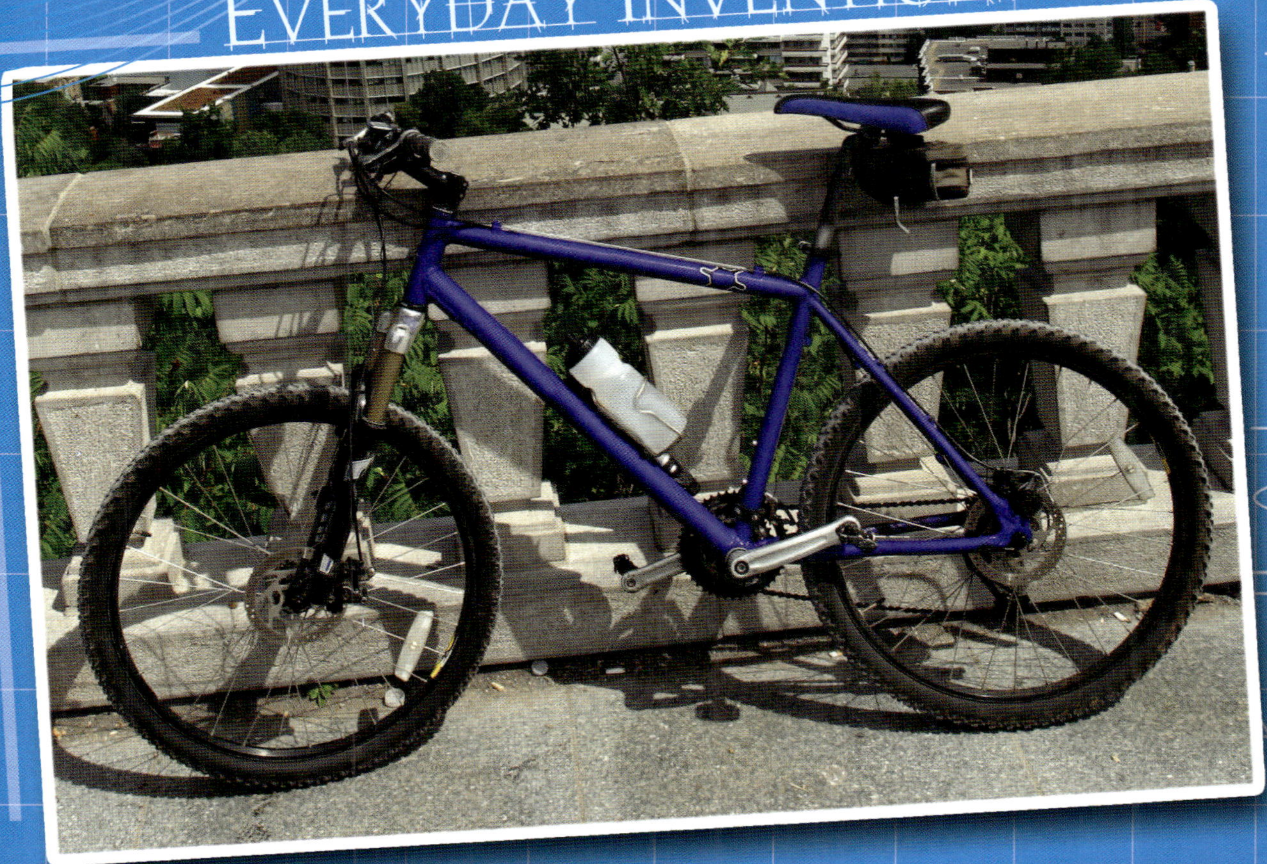

Kristin Petrie
ABDO Publishing Company

visit us at
www.abdopublishing.com

Published by ABDO Publishing Company, 8000 West 78th Street, Edina, Minnesota 55439. Copyright © 2009 by Abdo Consulting Group, Inc. International copyrights reserved in all countries. No part of this book may be reproduced in any form without written permission from the publisher. The Checkerboard Library™ is a trademark and logo of ABDO Publishing Company.

Printed in the United States.

Cover Photo: iStockphoto
Interior Photos: Alamy pp. 16, 22; AP Images pp. 18, 25, 27; Comstock p. 13; Corbis pp. 5, 9, 10, 15; iStockphoto pp. 1, 14, 15, 19, 24, 31; Megan M. Gunderson p. 16; Neil Klinepier pp. 16, 20–21, 29; Peter Arnold pp. 11, 17; PhotoEdit p. 28; Photo Researchers pp. 12, 19

Series Coordinator: Megan M. Gunderson
Editors: Rochelle Baltzer, Megan M. Gunderson
Art Direction & Cover Design: Neil Klinepier

Library of Congress Cataloging-in-Publication Data

Petrie, Kristin, 1970-
  Bicycles / Kristin Petrie.
     p. cm. -- (Everyday inventions)
  Includes bibliographical references and index.
  ISBN 978-1-60453-084-1
  1. Bicycles--Juvenile literature. I. Title.

TL412.P47 2009
629.227'2--dc22

2008001557

CONTENTS

Bicycles	4
Timeline	6
Bicycle Facts	7
Bicycle Evolution	8
Bits and Pieces	14
Pedaling	22
Roads to Mountains	24
A Bicycle Built for You	26
Healthy Travels	28
Glossary	30
Web Sites	31
Index	32

Bicycles

Do you have a bicycle? Lots of kids and adults do. In fact, more than 40 percent of Americans own a bicycle. In the Netherlands, more than 70 percent of people own one!

Bicycles are popular around the world for many reasons. These simple machines help us quickly get from place to place. They can go where cars can't go. Plus, they allow kids to be in the driver's seat!

Bicycles are good for more than just riding for fun. In busy cities, cyclists can zoom past traffic jams. And in the country, certain bicycles can take you on dirt paths and into wooded areas. Best of all, you are getting good exercise wherever you ride a bicycle.

Another great thing about bicycles is that they are simple machines. If yours breaks down, you may be able to fix it yourself!

Bicycling should be both fun and safe. Always wear a helmet! In many states, laws require this of riders under age 16.

Timeline

1790	The célérifère was invented.
1817	Baron Karl de Drais invented the draisienne, which had a steering bar attached to the front wheel.
1839	Kirkpatrick MacMillan added cranks that riders pushed back and forth with their feet.
1861	Pierre and Ernest Michaux created bicycle cranks that riders rotated in a circle.
1871	James Starley invented the Ariel, which had a large front wheel and a smaller back wheel.
1874	H.J. Lawson created a bicycle with a chain-driven back wheel.
1885	John Kemp Starley designed the Rover Safety model.
1888	John Boyd Dunlop introduced pneumatic tires for bicycles, creating a much smoother ride.
1980	The mountain bike was introduced.

Bicycle Facts

- Today, there are more than 1 billion bicycles in the world. That's more than double the number of cars!

- The Tour de France is one of the world's most challenging bicycle competitions. The race is held mostly in France for three weeks each June. During this time, racers travel more than 2,000 miles (3,200 km)! American cyclist Lance Armstrong won the race seven times in a row, a Tour de France record.

- The first motorcycle was a bicycle with a gasoline engine. German engineers Gottlieb Daimler and Wilhelm Maybach created it in 1885.

- In 2005, nearly 20 million bicycles were sold in the United States.

Bicycle Evolution

Did you know that early bicycles didn't have pedals? The bicycle has been around for many years. But, it has gone through several transformations. Like most inventions, the bicycle is a collection of ideas. Many great inventors contributed to the design of the bicycle we enjoy today.

Historians don't agree about who invented the very first bicycle. Some say Leonardo da Vinci drew a bicycle in the 1490s. But others say this drawing is a fake!

For a while, credit was given to France's Comte Médé de Sivrac. He invented a device similar to a bicycle in 1790. His design was called the célérifère.

The célérifère had two wheels of the same size. Its frame looked like a horse. The rider sat on what appeared to be the animal's back. Riders used their feet to push along the ground. This two-wheeled, human-powered device existed. But some people think Sivrac did not!

No matter who invented the célérifère, everyone agrees Baron Karl de Drais improved two-wheeled transportation in 1817. People still pushed themselves along with their feet. But, Drais added a steering bar to the front wheel. His invention was called the draisienne.

Drais called his invention a Laufmaschine, or "running machine." However, the name did not catch on.

A copy of Macmillan's bicycle

In 1839, Scottish blacksmith Kirkpatrick Macmillan became the first inventor to put pedals on a bicycle. His design included **cranks** that attached to the front. Riders pushed them back and forth with their feet. This action caused the back wheel to turn.

Soon, another brilliant design was tested. In 1861, Frenchman Pierre Michaux and his son Ernest added cranks that a rider rotated in a circle. These were attached to the front wheel. The invention's stiff design earned it the name boneshaker. It was a rough ride! More improvements were still needed.

In 1871, James Starley created a bicycle called the Ariel. It had a large front wheel and a smaller back wheel. The pedals were attached to the front wheel. Starley invented a gear that allowed

The penny-farthing was also called the ordinary bicycle.

the front wheel to turn twice every time a person pedaled. He also made improvements to the wheel spokes.

Soon, this bicycle became known as the penny-farthing. The design got its name from a large English coin called the penny and a smaller English coin called the farthing. Riding the penny-farthing required a lot of skill. Road **hazards** or fast braking could send a rider tumbling forward! But, it was very popular.

English inventor H.J. Lawson made bicycle news next. In 1874, he created an interesting design. Lawson's model had a chain that drove the back wheel of the bicycle. And unlike the penny-farthing, it had two wheels of the same size.

In 1885, another Englishman entered the scene. James Starley's nephew, John Kemp Starley, designed another bicycle with two wheels of the same size. This chain-driven bicycle was called the Rover Safety model. As it developed, the safety bicycle became the model for the bicycles we use today.

John Boyd Dunlop

Finally, there was a bicycle that was safe and affordable for everyone. The safety bicycle originally had solid rubber tires. But in 1888, John Boyd Dunlop introduced **pneumatic** tires. That year, he added them to his son's tricycle. This was the end of the boneshaker!

Mountain biking can take you places you've never seen before!

For more than 100 years, the basic design of the bicycle has not changed dramatically. Still, materials have improved so bicycles can be lighter and stronger. Most modern bicycles also have more than one gear and use **derailleurs**.

In 1980, the mountain bike was introduced. By 1993, these lightweight, strong, wide-tired bicycles were extremely popular. That year, 95 percent of U.S. bicycle sales were mountain bikes!

Bits and Pieces

Today's bicycles are made of many different parts. The stationary parts include the frame, the handlebars, and the seat. A bicycle frame is the base for all the other parts. The frame is made of **welded** tubes. Usually, these tubes form a diamond shape.

Handlebars are connected to the front of the frame. They come in a variety of shapes, but they all help riders steer and keep their balance. Flat handlebars are for mountain biking. Drop handlebars are for going fast and far on road bikes. Racers use aero bars to increase their speed.

A diamond-shaped bicycle frame's four points are near the handlebars, the pedals, the rear wheel hub, and the seat.

The style of seat, or saddle, depends on the bicycle's use and the rider's preference. Some saddles are small, while others are big and cushy. Most saddles have plastic bases. Some saddle coverings are made of leather. Others are padded with gel so they are softer to sit on. The seat post should be adjusted so the saddle is at a comfortable height.

Flat handlebars may have bar ends, which offer riders another hand position.

Drop handlebars offer a variety of hand positions.

Aero bars bring a racer's hands close together and offer armrests.

The moving parts of a bicycle include the pedals, the chain, and the gears. Pedals are the bicycle parts you put your feet on. There are flat, toe-clip, and clipless pedals.

Ordinary flat pedals are most popular with beginners and slower riders. Toe-clip pedals have what look like cages. These hold a rider's feet in place. They also give more power to pedaling. Last are clipless pedals. Riders wear special shoes to snap right into these.

Clipless pedals *(left)* require special shoes. They allow the rider to pedal stronger on the upstroke, like toe-clip pedals *(middle)*. They also leave the foot free, like flat pedals *(right)*.

  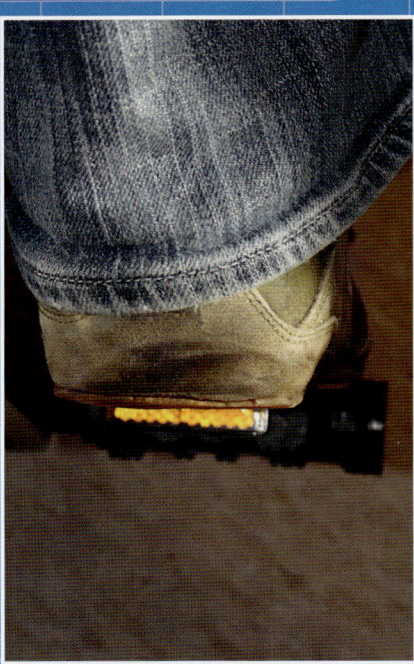

A bicycle chain is a series of metal links. Each link has a movable connection to the next. The links are designed to fit on the teeth of the rear **sprockets**, or cogs. They also fit on the teeth of the front sprockets, or chainwheels.

A bicycle's gears help you get more out of your pedaling. High gears produce a lot of power with every turn. On a flat road, you should use a high gear. This will let you go farther with less pedaling. Low gears make pedaling easier when going uphill. Front and rear **derailleurs** allow riders to switch between gears. Riders control these devices using levers on either the handlebars or the frame.

Most bicycles have two to three chainwheels and five to eight cogs. The chain travels on one chainwheel and one cog at all times.

Spokes attach a bicycle wheel's rim to its hub. They pull in on the wheel equally at all times. This keeps the wheel the correct shape, or true.

Last but not least are the bicycle's wheels, tires, and brakes. A bicycle wouldn't be much use without its wheels. Bicycle wheels consist of a rim and a **hub**, which are connected by spokes. Spokes are made of strong materials, such as stainless steel.

Tires are attached to the wheel rims. Thanks to air-filled tires, biking is enjoyable. Tires take on the bumps in the road so your body doesn't have to. And, their **treads** help stabilize your bicycle in mud or on wet surfaces.

Your bicycle's brakes help you stop. A rider controls the brakes using levers on the handlebars. These connect to the brakes by cables. When riders pull on the brake levers, they are pulling on the cables. This action pulls on the brake arms, which causes the brake shoes to press against the wheel rims. The pressure slows your bicycle tires and allows you to stop.

There are several different kinds of brakes. Centerpull caliper brakes pull on the brake arms from above the wheel. Sidepull caliper brakes pull on both brake arms from one side. Cantilever brakes pull on the brake arms separately. All of these rim brakes are located at the top of a bicycle's wheels.

CENTERPULL CALIPER BRAKES

CANTILEVER BRAKES

SIDEPULL CALIPER BRAKES

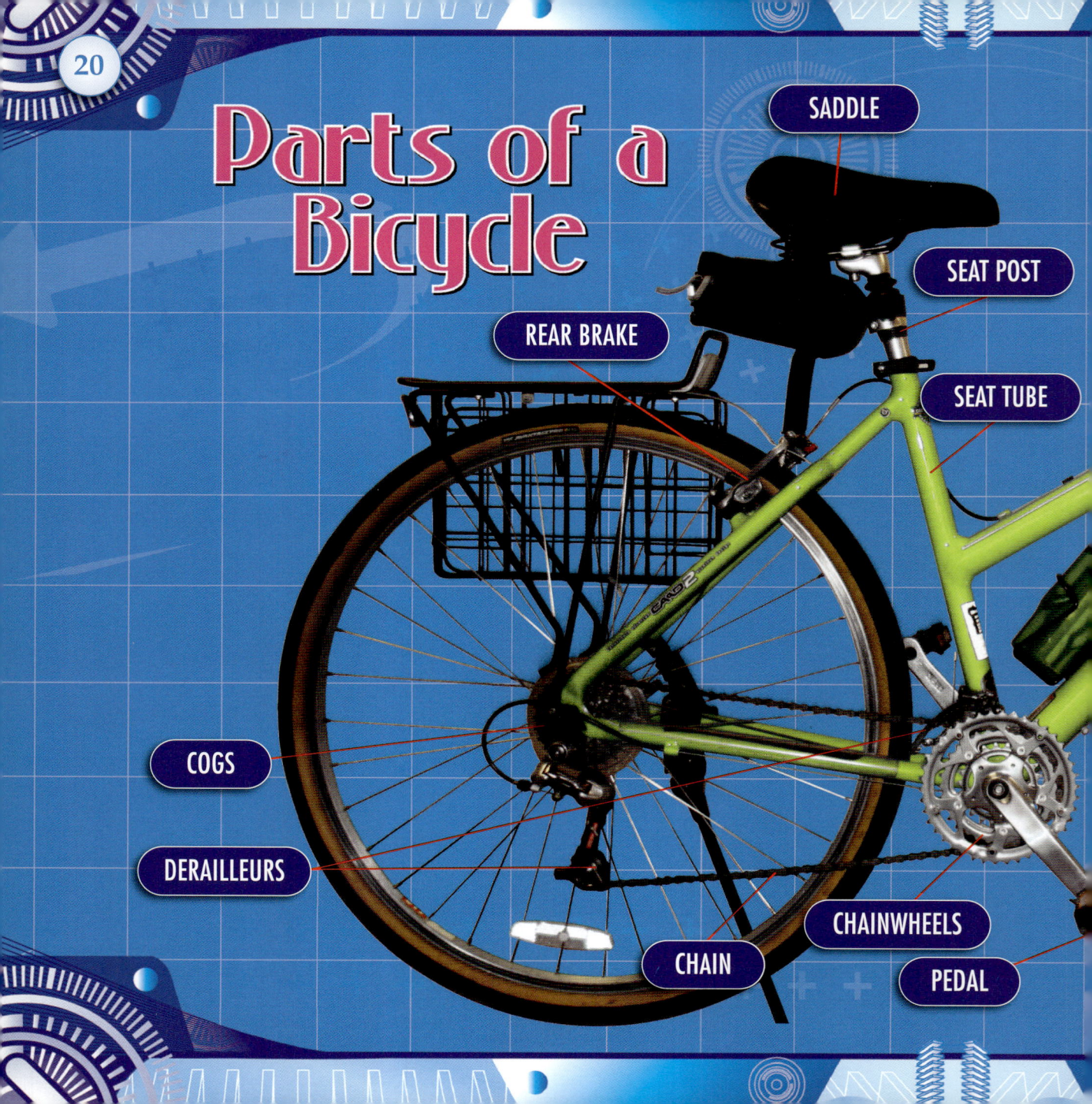

Pedaling

How do all these parts work? Let's start with the pedals. Place one foot on a pedal. Push off the ground with your other foot. When you get enough speed, you can use the other pedal, too.

Your forward motion must now be continued. Otherwise, you may end up on the ground! Your pedaling moves the **crank**. The crank has one or more chainwheels.

Everyone loses their balance at some point while riding a bicycle. That is part of the reason helmets are such a vital part of cycling!

BICYCLE RIDING SHOULD BE SAFE AS WELL AS FUN! FOLLOWING A FEW SIMPLE RULES WILL HELP YOU HAVE THE BEST POSSIBLE CYCLING EXPERIENCE.

- When riding on the street, always ride on the right side of the road. Stop at all stop signs and red lights, just like cars do.

- Always wear a helmet to protect your head. Never wear baggy clothing, because it can get caught in your bicycle. And remember, light-colored clothing makes you more visible to others.

- Drink plenty of water before, during, and after a long ride. Some bicycles even come equipped with a water bottle holder on the frame.

- Before every ride, inspect your bicycle's main parts. Make sure the tires are properly inflated and the brakes work. Check that the frame, wheels, and other parts are not bent.

- Keep your bicycle safe by keeping it clean! Wash away dirt and debris using a hose, soapy water, and a rag. Also, clean and relubricate the chain whenever dirt builds up.

The chainwheel is a toothy disk that turns as you pedal. It pulls the chain with it. The chain is also connected to one or more cogs. These cogs are connected to the rear wheel. When a cog turns, your rear wheel turns, too. Steer with your handlebars, and away you go. Bicycling is a very **efficient** way to travel!

Roads to Mountains

If you know where you want to ride, choosing a bicycle is easy! Road bikes are for speed, exercise, and recreational riding on hard surfaces. They have narrow tires, drop handlebars, and lightweight metal frames.

Mountain bikes are made to handle rough surfaces. So, they have thicker frames and big tires with heavy **treads**. **Hybrids** are similar to mountain bikes, but lighter. They are meant for both road and off-road cycling. Many recreational riders use these bicycles.

Bicycle motocross (BMX) bikes have small frames and small wheels. They first appeared in the 1970s.

BMX bikes were designed for jumps!

A recumbent bicycle's handlebars may be down next to the seat or out in front.

BMX bikes are popular for racing on dirt tracks and performing tricks.

Recumbent bicycles allow riders to sit back in a seat with their legs stretched out in front. The pedals are near the front tire. Some recumbent bicycles have a **streamlined** outer shell. This allows riders to reach speeds of 60 miles per hour (100 km/h)!

Tandem bicycles carry two riders. Riders have their own handlebars, but only the front rider steers. There is one chain driven by two sets of pedals. The riders pedal together for extra speed. Teamwork is key!

A Bicycle Built for You

There are plenty of careers in the world of bicycles. Designers are at the beginning of the bicycle-making process. Each year, they continue their quest for faster, stronger bicycles.

After the designs are complete, bicycle manufacturers take over. They build bicycles based on the designs. Then, the new bicycles hit the showroom. There, salespeople promote each bicycle model's great design and extra features.

Got a flat tire? Many bicycle books offer instructions for repairing your own bicycle. But sometimes, bicycles need professional repair. Repairers will keep your bicycle in tip-top shape. You can even take it in for a yearly tune-up. This care keeps bicycles safe, fun, and easy to ride.

Countless other people use bicycles for their jobs. Bicycle racers compete worldwide. Some messengers use bicycles to quickly get around cities. And kids use bicycles to deliver newspapers!

Delivering newspapers means even kids can use bicycles for their jobs!

Healthy Travels

Bicycles are fun! They are also a great way to get around. Their small design allows bicycles to fit where cars cannot. Best of all, you don't need a license to ride a bicycle! They allow you to get around even if you are too young to drive a car.

Bicycles are also affordable to purchase and maintain. You don't have to pay for gasoline, because your own strength powers your bicycle! There rarely are expensive tune-ups or repairs. And, you don't need to pay for parking.

Bicycling can help you learn skills such as how to repair a flat tire. It is also a great way to spend time with friends and family.

Bicycling is also good for the planet. Cars may give off dangerous fumes, but bicycles do not. By riding a bicycle, you are promoting a healthier world. Bicycle riding is great exercise, it is fun, and it gives you freedom. Enjoy!

Placing the left hand straight out indicates a left turn.

HAND SIGNALS ARE AN IMPORTANT PART OF BICYCLE SAFETY. RIDERS SHOULD ALWAYS SIGNAL WHEN THEY ARE GOING TO TURN OR STOP.

Placing the left hand up at a right angle indicates a right turn.

Pointing the left hand down indicates a stop or slowing down.

GLOSSARY

crank - a device that when turned, transfers motion from one part of a machine to another.
derailleur (dih-RAY-luhr) - a device that moves a bicycle chain from one sprocket to another. This allows a rider to shift gears.
efficient - wasting little time or energy.
hazard - a source of danger.
hub - the central part of something circular. The center of a bicycle wheel where all the spokes attach is a hub.
hybrid - combining two or more functions or ways of operation.
pneumatic (nu-MA-tihk) - filled with compressed air.
sprocket - a wheel with teeth that hook into links in a chain.
streamlined - designed to reduce drag or resistance to motion when moving through air or water.
tread - the part of a wheel or a tire that comes in contact with the road surface. Tread also refers to the grooves and markings on the surface of a tire.
weld - to join metal parts using heat.

WEB SITES

To learn more about bicycles, visit ABDO Publishing Company on the World Wide Web at **www.abdopublishing.com**. Web sites about bicycles are featured on our Book Links page. These links are routinely monitored and updated to provide the most current information available.

INDEX

A
Ariel 10, 11

B
BMX bike 24, 25
boneshaker 10, 12
brakes 18, 19

C
careers 26, 27
célérifère 8, 9
chain 12, 16, 17, 23, 25
chainwheels 17, 22, 23
cogs 17, 23
cranks 10, 22

D
derailleurs 13, 17
Drais, Karl de 9
draisienne 9
Dunlop, John Boyd 12

F
frame 8, 14, 17, 24

G
gears 10, 13, 16, 17

H
handlebars 14, 17, 18, 23, 24, 25
hub 18
hybrid bicycle 24

L
Lawson, H.J. 12
Leonardo da Vinci 8

M
Macmillan, Kirkpatrick 10
Michaux, Ernest 10
Michaux, Pierre 10
mountain bike 13, 14, 24

P
pedals 8, 10, 16, 22, 25
penny-farthing 11, 12

R
racing 14, 25, 27
recumbent bicycle 25
repair 4, 26, 28
rim 18, 19
road bike 14, 24
Rover Safety model 12

S
seat 14, 15, 25
Sivrac, Médé de 8
spokes 11, 18
Starley, James 10, 11, 12
Starley, John Kemp 12

T
tandem bicycle 25
tires 12, 13, 18, 19, 24, 25, 26

W
wheels 8, 9, 10, 11, 12, 18, 19, 23, 24